A Pet's Life

Dogs

Anita Ganeri

www.heinemannlibrary.co.uk
Visit our website to find out more information about Heinemann Library books.

To order:
 Phone +44 (0) 1865 888066
Fax +44 (0) 1865 314091
Visit www.heinemannlibrary.co.uk

Heinemann Library is an imprint of Capstone Global Library Limited, a company incorporated in England and Wales having its registered office at 7 Pilgrim Street, London, EC4V 6LB – Registered company number: 6695582

Edited by Charlotte Guillain and Harriet Milles
Designed by Joanna Hinton-Malivoire
Picture research by Liz Alexander
Production by Victoria Fitzgerald
Originated by Chroma Graphics (Overseas) Pte. Ltd
Printed and bound in China by South China Printing Company Ltd.

ISBN 978 0 43117788 5 (hardback)
13 12 11 10 09
10 9 8 7 6 5 4 3 2 1

ISBN 978 0 4311 7795 3 (paperback)
13 12 11 10 09
10 9 8 7 6 5 4 3 2 1

British Library Cataloguing in Publication Data
Ganeri, Anita, 1961-
   Dogs. - 2nd ed. - (A pet's life) (Heinemann first library)
   1. Dogs - Juvenile literatre
   I. Title
   636.7
A full catalogue record for this book is available from the British Library.

Acknowledgements
We would like to thank the following for permission to reproduce photographs:
Alamy p. **22** (© TNT MAGAZINE); Ardea pp. **7**, **14** (© John Daniels); © Capstone Global Library Ltd. pp. **8** (Mark Farrell), **19**, **25** (Trevor Clifford), **5**, **12**, **13**, **16**, **17**, **20**, **24**, **27** (Tudor Photography); Getty Images p. **23** (The Image Bank/LWA); Masterfile p. **15** (Alison Barnes Martin); Photolibrary p. **18** (Juniors Bildarchiv); RSPCA p. **26** (Colin Seddon); Shutterstock p. **4** (© Eric Isselée); Warren Photographic pp. **6**, **9**, **11**, **21** (Jane Burton), **10**.

Cover photograph reproduced with permission of Photolibrary (Juniors Bildarchiv).

The publishers would like to thank Rob Lee for his assistance in the preparation of this book.

Contents

Any words appearing in the text in bold, **like this**, are explained in the Glossary.

What do dogs look like?

Dogs come in many different sizes and colours. They can have long or short hair. Most dogs have tails that they can wag. Dogs make wonderful pets.

Dogs can be very big, or very tiny!

This picture shows the different parts of a dog's body. You can see what each part is used for.

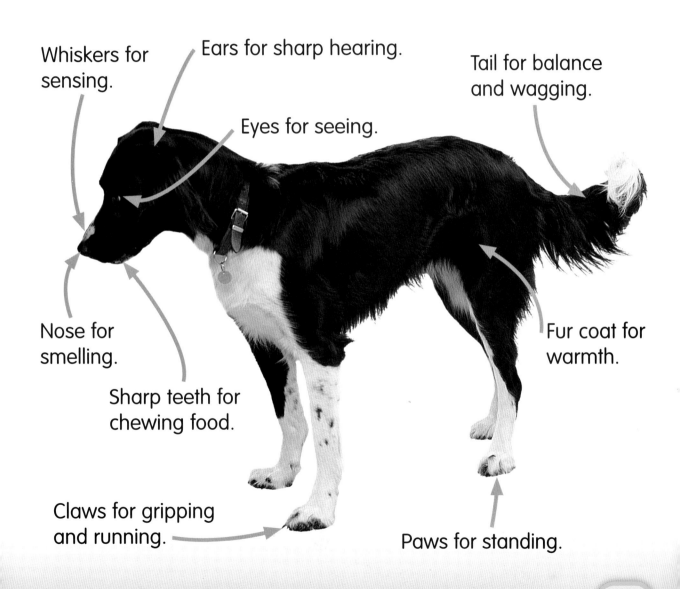

Whiskers for sensing.

Ears for sharp hearing.

Tail for balance and wagging.

Eyes for seeing.

Nose for smelling.

Fur coat for warmth.

Sharp teeth for chewing food.

Claws for gripping and running.

Paws for standing.

Dog babies

Baby dogs are called puppies. Small dogs may have up to six puppies in a **litter**. Big dogs may have as many as twelve puppies.

A mother dog feeds her puppies on milk.

At eight weeks old, the **vet** will give your puppy **injections** to stop it becoming ill.

Puppies must stay with their mother until they are at least eight weeks old. Then they are old enough to be chosen as pets.

Choosing your dog

Animal shelters have many dogs and puppies that need loving homes. You might want to pick an older dog instead of a puppy.

The people at the shelter will help you to pick the right dog for you.

Choose a lively, happy dog with a glossy coat, clean ears, and bright eyes. A cold, wet nose is a sign that a dog is healthy.

Look for an active dog that is happy to see you.

Growing up

As your puppy grows up, you will get to know it very well. When it wags its tail, it means that it is pleased to see you.

Bowing like this means that your dog wants to play.

Dogs and puppies are fun, but they need a lot of care. You will need to look after your pet for the whole of its life. This could be from about 13 to 18 years.

If you look after your dog, you will quickly become its best friend.

Things to get ready

Get everything ready before you bring your new pet home. Your dog needs a bed with a washable blanket. It needs bowls for food and water, and toys to play with.

A chew-proof dog bed is best for your pet.

Your dog must wear a collar and tag. The tag should have your name and address on it, in case your pet gets lost. Always put your dog on a lead when you take it for a walk.

You should put your dog's name on the tag, too.

Welcome home

Put your dog's bed in a quiet place, away from draughts. Show your dog where its bed is and leave it to settle in for a while.

A dog might feel lonely on its first night in its new home.

Cats and dogs can get on well once they get to know each other.

If you have other pets, introduce them slowly to your dog. Don't leave them alone together at first. After a while, they should become good friends.

Feeding time

Adult dogs need one or two meals a day. Puppies need three or four smaller meals. You can feed your dog on dry food or tinned dog food mixed with cereal or dog biscuits.

Feed your dog or puppy at the same time every day.

Chews are good for cleaning your dog's teeth.

Make sure that your dog always has fresh water to drink. You can sometimes give your dog a biscuit or chew as a special treat.

Playing with your dog

Dogs like toys that they can chew. You can buy dog toys from a pet shop. Buy well-made toys that are too big for your dog to swallow.

Dogs love to play games of fetch and catch with balls and frisbees.

Dogs need lots of exercise to stay healthy.

You should take your dog for a walk twice a day. Make sure you always clear up any **dog mess**. Ask an adult to teach you how to do this cleanly and safely.

Training your dog

All dogs and puppies need to be trained. You should teach your dog to come when you call its name, and to sit down when you tell it to.

You can train your dog at home or take it to a dog training class.

If your puppy needs the toilet, put it down on some newspaper at first.

Puppies need to learn to go to the toilet outside. Put some newspaper down for your puppy. Slowly move the newspaper closer to the door. It will soon learn to go outside.

Family pet

If you cannot take your dog on holiday, you may be able to leave it with a friend or neighbour. Otherwise you can put your dog in **boarding kennels**.

Boarding kennels are like hotels for dogs.

Your dog can become your family's best friend!

Older dogs become part of the family. Your dog will enjoy taking walks, going on holiday, and playing with you.

A healthy dog

If you look after your dog, it should stay fit and healthy. Take your dog to the **vet** if you are worried about it.

If your dog does not want to eat or play, it might be unwell. Take it to the vet to find out what is wrong.

The vet can also clip your dog's nails so that it doesn't scratch itself.

You should take your dog to the vet once a year for a check-up. The vet will check your dog all over to make sure that it is healthy.

Old age

As your dog gets older, it might not be able to see or hear as well as before. Your dog may want to sleep more often.

An older dog might not want to walk too far.

It can be very upsetting when your pet dies. Try not to be too sad. Just remember all the happy times that you shared.

Caring for your dog will help you learn how to treat animals properly.

Useful tips

- If you want to pick up your puppy, put one hand under its chest and the other hand under its bottom.

- **Groom** your dog every day to keep its coat clean and shiny, and to get any old hairs out.

- Ask your **vet** what medicines you should use to stop your dog from getting fleas and worms.

- Never leave dogs in a car on a warm day, even with a window open. Dogs can die in hot cars.

- Don't let your puppy outside before it has its first **injections**. It might catch a **disease** from another dog.

- Dogs like company. It is not fair to get a dog if you are going to leave it on its own for a long time each day.

Fact file

- All pet dogs are **related** to wolves. Wolves were probably first kept as pets about 12,000 years ago.

- In ancient China, people worshipped dogs as gods. They thought dogs scared away evil spirits.

- There are about 200 million pet dogs around the world.

- The heaviest **breeds** of pet dog are St Bernards and Old English mastiffs.

- The oldest pet dog known was an Australian cattle-dog called Bluey. He died in 1939, at the age of 29.

- Dogs have an amazing sense of smell. A dog can smell things more than one thousand times better than you can.

Glossary

animal shelter place where lost or unwanted animals are looked after and found new homes

boarding kennels place where you can leave your dog when you go on holiday

breed kind or type of animal

disease illness

dog mess dog poo. Dog mess can carry diseases so you must always clean up after your dog and wash your hands afterwards.

groom brush and clean your dog's coat

injection medicine that is given by a vet to stop dogs catching diseases

litter group of puppies

related being part of the same family

vet specially trained animal doctor

More information

Books to read

First Pets: Dogs and Puppies, K. Starke (Usborne Publishing, 2nd ed., 2004)

Puppy Training for Kids, Sarah Whitehead (Barron's Educational series, 2001)

My Pet: Puppy, Honor Head (Belitha Press, 2000)

RSPCA Pet Guide: Care for your Puppy, (Collins, 2004)

Websites

www.rspca.org.uk
The website of The Royal Society for the Prevention of Cruelty to Animals in Britain.

www.pethealthcare.co.uk
Information about keeping and caring for pets.

www.petlink.com.au
Information about being a good pet owner.

Index